Wood Carving

Yesterday & Today in America

Hand crafted cow's head from the barn of S. L. Carpenter of West Earl, Lancaster County, Pennsylvania. His sign noted, "General dealer in hides, tallow, etc. 1890"

The carved horse is from Maryland and the bull from the mountains of West Virginia. These items are on display in the Folk Craft Museum, Witmer, Pennsylvania.

APPLIED ARTS PUBLISHERS

Third Printing LEBANON, PA. 17042

ISBN 0-911410-41-4

AGE-OLD TRADITION & CONTEMPORARY CRAFT

Sugar Molds

SUGAR WATER was obtained by tapping the trees and the liquid was boiled down into syrup or sugar in those regions where the climate was appropriate and the maple trees were abundant. Early settlers from New England southward to western Virginia depended on this "tree molasses" for much of their sweetening. Boiled into a thick syrup and poured into molds to harden, it made delicious sugar candy.

The hand-carved molds shown include a rare cow carved in pine from New England and the five below are from Pennsylvania, carried to Iowa about thirty years ago. The two large specimens are maple and the smaller ones are carved in pine.

Wooden sugar molds are not common because tin became available in the first half of the last century and the little tin molds were reasonable in price and more convenient to clean and store.

Upper: Full-size maple sugar mold with a pipe and coffee pot design. From Highland County, Virginia, where an annual Maple Festival is held each spring.

Below: Hardwood sugar molds portray chicks and farm animals, each design makes a small piece of sugar candy. The three specimens just below are from Iowa and the one at the bottom is from West Virginia.

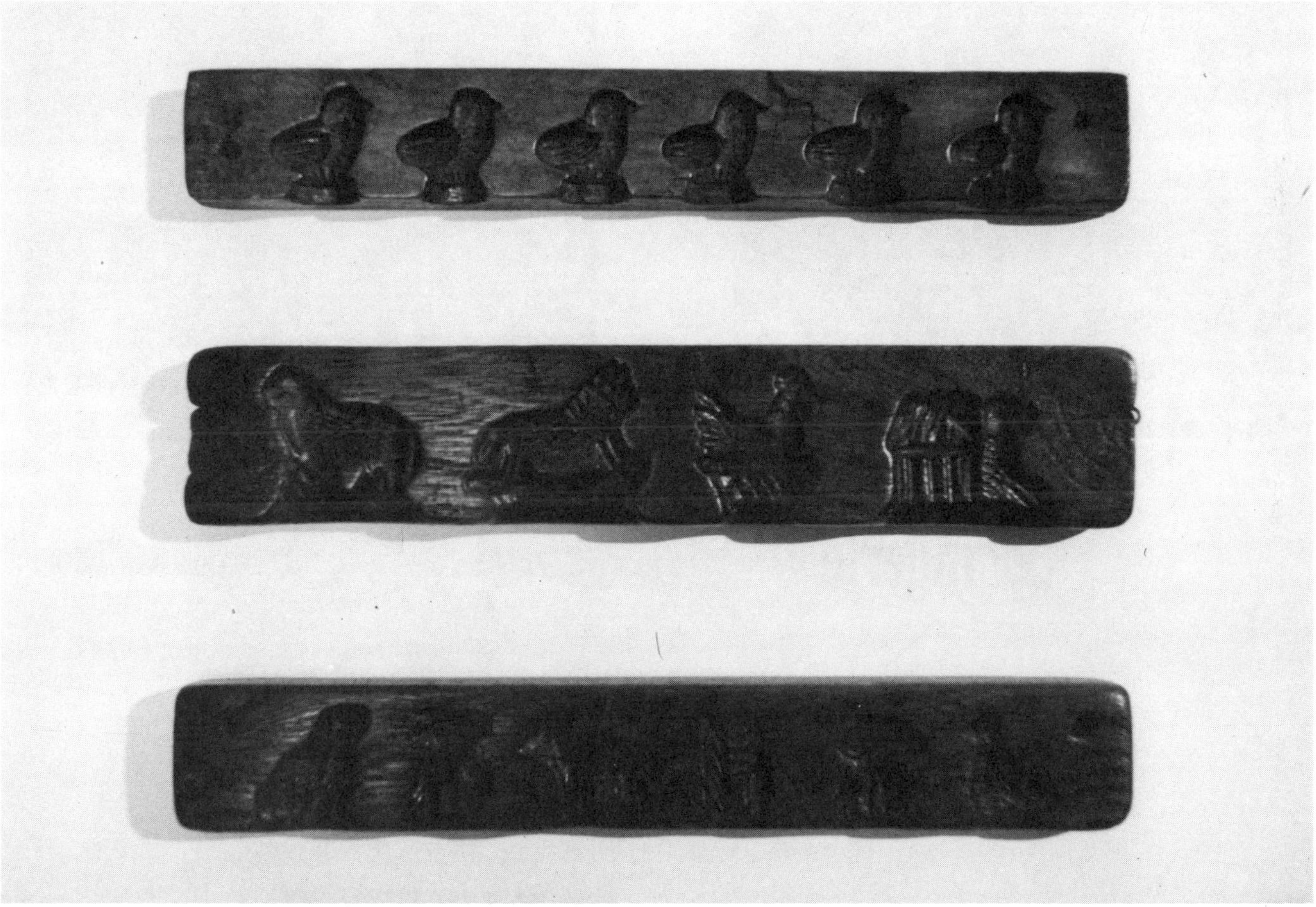

Springerle

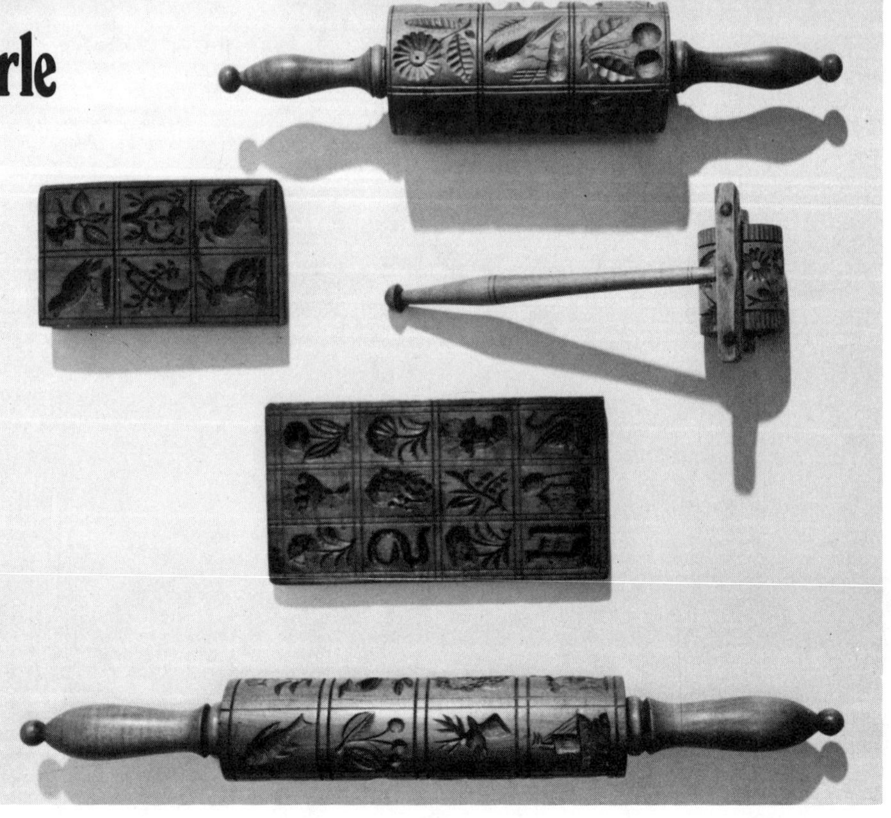

Why Springerle?

ONE of the most interesting decorative utilitarian wooden objects is the *springerle* board. These carved boards date back to around 1750 when a Holland Dutch carver named Springerly developed such equipment for making Christmas cookies. Cookies made on such boards with various designs and figures were often added to the tree!

Specimens on these pages include a twelve-design board (both sides) from a rural German community in northeastern Iowa and one (below) from a German area of rural Wisconsin. The carved roller is from Wisconsin.

The rooster cookie mold from Western Maryland measures 8″ x 13″.

Cookie Boards

TWO COOKIE BOARDS from Holland, Michigan, appear as folk carvings but were likely made in the Old World. Such objects were brought by immigrants or sent from the Old World by relatives as gifts to loved ones across the sea. Nevertheless, skilled carvers migrated to America where they perpetuated, when time was available, the traditional hand-work of the homeland.

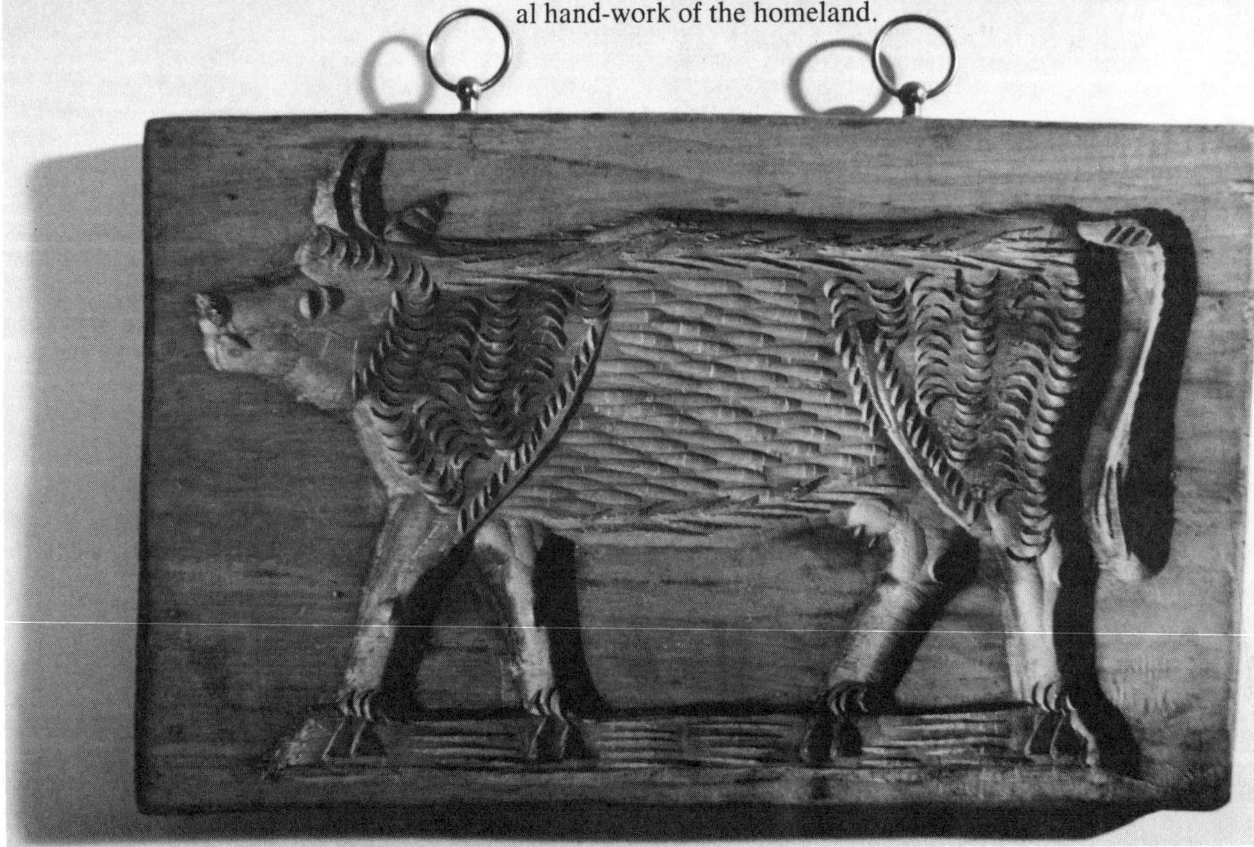

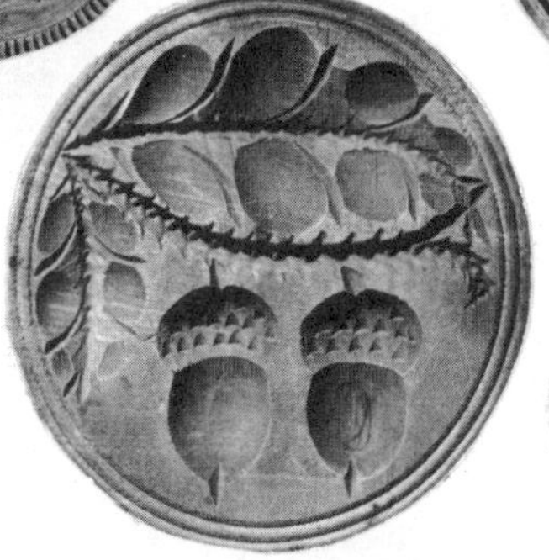

Butter Prints

BUTTER PRINTS were made in an assortment of shapes (circular, semi-circular, square, oblong and six-sided) and in a variety of sizes (individual pats, half-pound, pound and two-pound) and they were carved with hundreds of different designs. When imprinted on butter the intaglio designs stand out in relief.

Such objects were made in Europe as long ago as the mid-eighteenth century. Today considered a form of rural folk art, many of the later case mold types were actually machine made.

Specimens illustrated are from the area of rural Virginia northward to New England.

Turned and Decorated

IN ADDITION to carved objects, there were those that were turned on a hand or foot-powered lathe. A variety of small pieces—mortars, sugar buckets, saffron and spice holders, match and pin holders and egg cups were created on the lathe.

LEHNWARE

Perhaps the most publicized maker of such objects was Joseph Lehn (1798-1892), a farmer near Lititz, Pennsylvania, who whiled away the long winter months turning wood into small objects from his lathe. He decorated these pieces with the traditional designs of the Pennsylvania Germans in soft but gay colors. His brother, George, made similar pieces which he usually marked on the bottom: "G. Lehn."

The pieces on display (left) at the Pennsylvania Farm Museum are all examples of the Lehn's of Lititz and this type object is often referred to today as Lehnware.

During the early part of the present century, others produced pieces very similar to those of the Lehn brothers.

The turned and carved piece below was made by an unknown craftsman in the Shenandoah Valley.

One contemporary woodworker in the "Lehn tradition" is Robert F. Lausch, of Ephrata, Pennsylvania. As early as 20 to 25 years ago, Lausch turned and hand-decorated the two pieces (upper right). Here he is carving a butter mold. Some of his earlier works are bringing "top dollar" at antique sales. Lausch became a skilled wood turner and carver at an early age under the watchful eyes of his father and grandfather who were both skilled craftsmen.

Jacob Brubaker made the three turned pieces below—a covered saffron container, covered pinholder, an egg cup. They are decorated with the strawberry motif, a design he favored on much of his work.

Ed Longenecker, of Lititz, Pa., is a skilled cabinet maker. As another worker in this tradition, he turns "Lehn-type" ware as a hobby, and produced the undecorated egg cup and saffron cup shown in the lower right.

Robert Lausch at work

Whittling-

CARVING WITH A KNIFE

WHITTLING is an unusually simple and inexpensive leisure activity—all that is needed is a pocketknife, a whetstone to keep the blade sharp, and of course, a piece of wood. It can be done inside, outdoors, or wherever the carver might be comfortable.

Carvings have been made by the most primitive peoples around the world and frequently with the most simple of knives.

The art of whittling is a handy form of self-expression—but the beginner will perhaps benefit from suggestions and hints, including the selection of a knife and the type of wood to use.

The Knife

A good grade of steel knife will remain sharp and not chip when a knot is struck in the wood. The handle should be smooth and three or more inches long. (Fancy or decorated handles may look nice, but they have no functional value for a carver.) The good whittling knife should have sturdy side plates with strong rivets to keep the blades from becoming loose and wobbly. Stiff strong springs keep the blades from closing accidently while carving, and help avoid the common accidents of the carver—cut fingers!

A three-blade knife offers multiple-use; the large blade for rough heavy cutting, medium blade for

Fire destroyed Frank Updegrove's 49-year collection of circus-related carvings in 1955. He then turned to carving animals, some of which are shown above. This Boyertown Pennsylvania Dutchman began carving when employed by Ringling Brothers. In recent years he has demonstrated his carving skills at festivals in Hershey and Kutztown, Pa.

general whittling, small blade for fine detail work.

With experience, and after various types of objects are carved, the whittler may find a need for one or more specialized knives. These can often be made by grinding down other tools—old saw blades, paper openers, palette knives and similar hand-me-down objects.

The blades should be kept sharp. Lay the blade flat on a whetstone and draw the knife back and forth over the stone, first one side and then the other. Blades can also be made razor-sharp by use of carborundum cloth.

The Wood

The beginner will find softwood to be the most suitable. Perhaps the most appropriate softwoods are *sugar pine* or *white pine*. These have little grain, few knots, and are inexpensive. Other good softwoods that are quite readily carved are *poplar* and *basswood*—any native woods that are free of resin and pitch can be used.

The softest woods are recommended for a beginner—with the exception of *balsa,* because it is too soft to hold up well and crushes easily under pressure.

Once the art of whittling is achieved, the challenge of hardwoods and other materials (such as bone or horn) will perhaps be too much for the carver to resist!

Blocking Out

After choosing a subject, most carvers cut away large portions of the unnecessary block—this is often referred to as "blocking out."

A sketch of the subject is prepared in outline and in the size of the object to be carved. This is dupli-

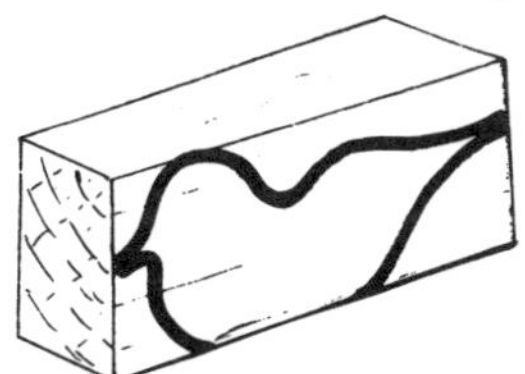

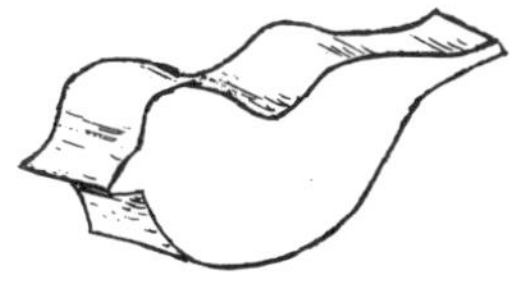

cated in silhouette on the *side* of the block. Excess wood is then cut away. A saw (jig, band or coping) is the most commonly used tool for this task.

The second step in blocking is completed by drawing a line down the center and sketching the outline of the shape of the subject as viewed from the *top,* again removing the unnecessary wood.

A third step involves cutting away excess wood from the *corners* and *edges*. This leaves the block

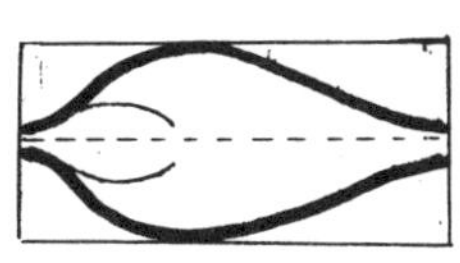

ready to be completed by hand with a knife.

A few old-time whittlers claim that *all* the work should be by hand and only with a knife—"or it just ain't whittlin!" But contemporary carvers take the position that the finished piece is "hand-carved" because that is the part of the work that shows the craftsman's skill—not the shavings and scraps!

Using the Knife

For rough whittling the knife must be held firmly. The hand holding the wood should always be back of the blade and away from the cutting edge. Hold the knife with the handle in the middle of

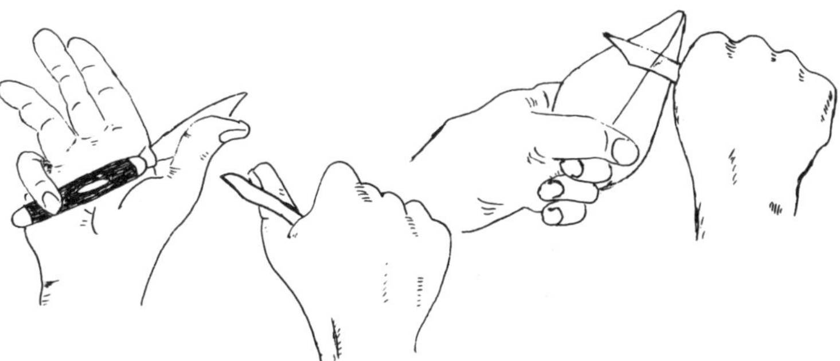

the palm—the back of the blade should set in the crotch formed by the index finger and thumb. Strokes should always be away from a carver.

In fine cutting, the thumb is generally rested on some part of the wood—the forefinger closes around the base of the blade and the thumb helps steady

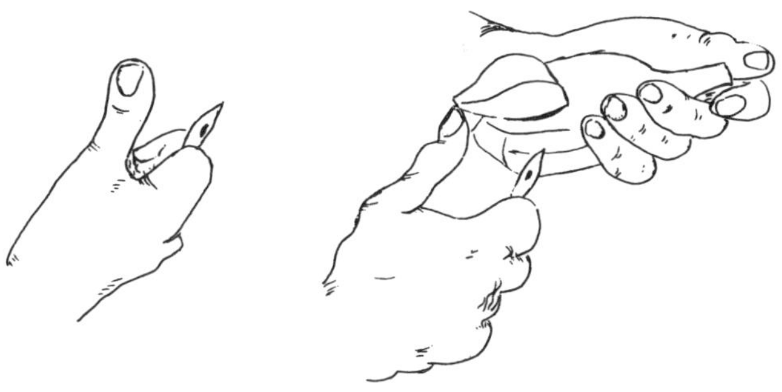

the blade and assists in pulling the blade through the wood toward the whittler.

These two basic holds become natural with time and experience and the individual whittler will develop his own variations depending on the situation.

Whittling simply cannot be done well with a dull knife—in fact, a razor-sharp blade slips less often than does a dull blade, so the knife should be kept sharpened. A handy and inexpensive device for this is made by simply tacking a piece of carborundum cloth or emery to a wooden strip—sharpen the blade by drawing it across the cloth in one direction. Complete the process by drawing the blade across a leather strop fastened to a wood strip—this keeps the blade honed.

Wooden Decoys

Canadian goose (above) by Thomas Marshall, Smith Island, Maryland. The three (below) represent a New England type decoy; the pintail and sleeping black duck are from the Chesapeake Bay.

CARVED wooden wildfowl decoys were originally part of the hunter's equipment, to lure birds from the sky to a spot near the hunter. Decoy making was common along the major waterways and flyways where migrating ducks and geese rested or wintered. Makers of decoys were often fishermen who crafted them during the long off-season winter months.

Ducks dominate the decoys but geese and some shore birds were also carved. Thousands were created for market gunners who used as many as 500 decoys in a single stand. A typical gunner had a rig of 30 to 35 decoys.

By the turn of the century several makers were advertising their decoys, selling them for between 25¢ and 40¢ each. By the 1930's decoys were beginning to be viewed as a form of folk art and contemporary carvers now produce them as "decorative" art.

The montage (FACING PAGE) portrays decoys characteristic of the carving traditions of the Illinois River, Barnegat Bay, the Chesapeake, and upper New York. They range from folk art to factory type. Included are contemporary carvings by Jim Pierce of Havre-de-Grace, Maryland, and Ed Sweet, Ogdensburg, N.Y.

A Canadian goose from the eastern shore of Virginia flanked by a black crow from Delaware.

Passenger pigeon from Illinois; black ducks by Dave Watson of Chincoteague Island; and three ducks by Ira Hudson of eastern Virginia. The black crow (right) is from New Jersey.

Scrimshaw

SCRATCH ENGRAVING on bone, horn and ivory has been known since the 11th century, and it is not surprising that scratch decorations on objects ranging from powder horns to corset busks have been made in America.

The sea-going folk of the northeastern coast—whalers in particular—at sea for long periods of time, fashioned objects from materials at hand. One form is *scrimshaw*.

Scrimshaw engravings portray any number of subjects but most common are the scenes depicting whaling ships, spouting mammals and the hunt, scratched in whale teeth or whalebone. These were non-utilitarian objects often given as gifts to loved ones upon return from a long voyage.

Inscribed and carved objects for use were also made. Net-making and repairing implements were commonly carved objects, several types are shown below.

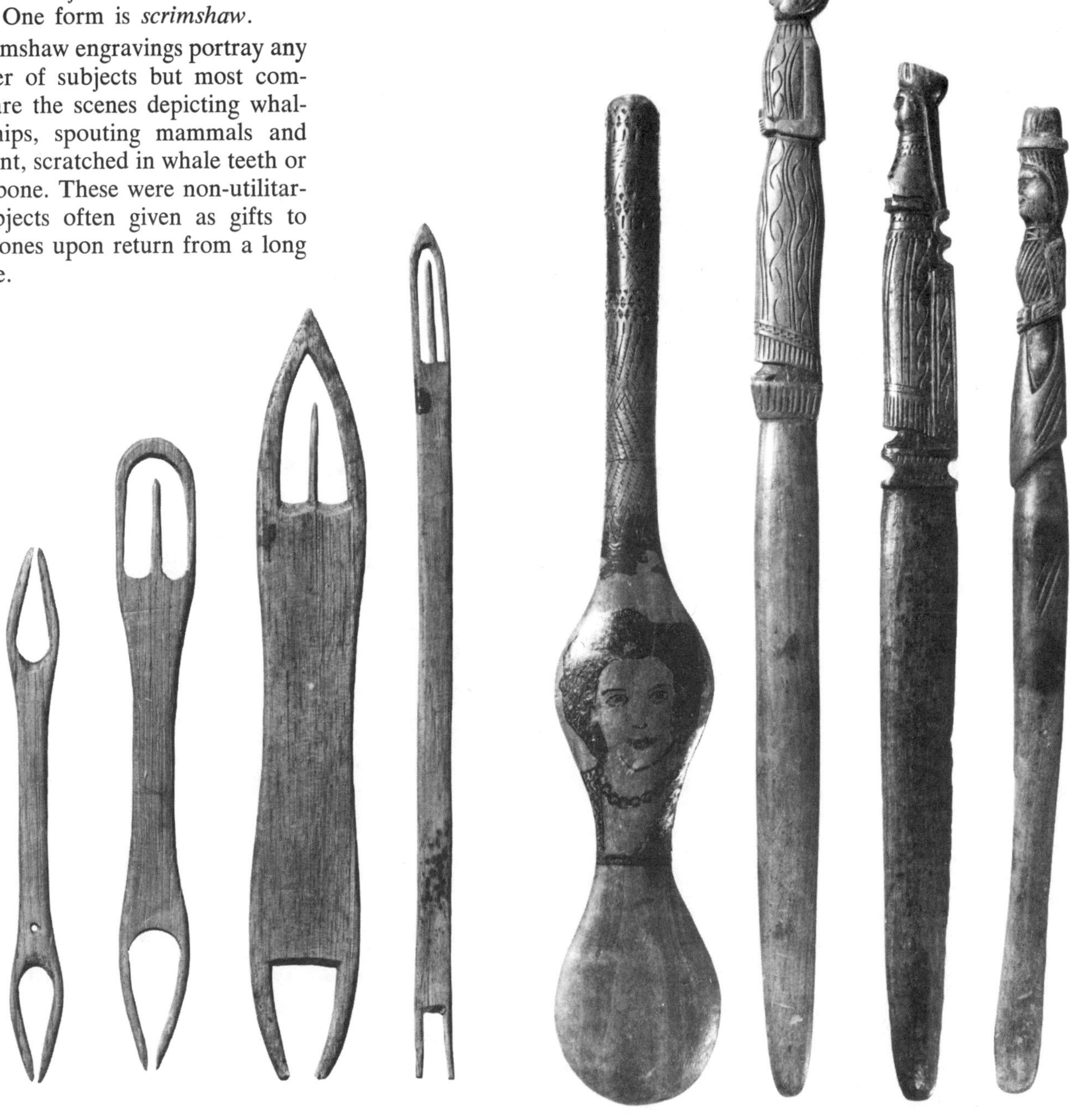

Apple wood pig and bull. The horse was carved on walnut.

Blocks courtesy of the Historical Society of the Cocalico Valley, Pennsylvania.

Said to be cut by William Kafroth, late 19th century.

Printing Blocks

THE LEAST RECOGNIZED of the folk craftsmen were those who carved the early wood blocks used for printing handbills, posters, broadsides and newspaper illustrations. These early blocks reflect the economic emphasis of the time and showed primarily scenes of rural life. Usually coarse in effect, the non-printed areas were gouged out with a knife on relatively soft wood. Wood *engravings* are not considered a handcraft—they were usually professionally done with a graver on the end grain of hard wood.

Since the product was associated with the printing craft, the rise of photo-engraving and improved technology rendered hand-made wooden blocks obsolete. They were often disposed of to make room for new equipment—the result has been the disappearance of most of the early wood blocks.

Illustrations on the adjoining page were made by William Kafroth who was born about 1830 and worked for a daily newspaper in his early years. Later he worked for rural weeklies—*Weekly Graphic, Denver Press,* and *West Earl Banner* and was an itinerant, travelling from village to village until his death at nearly ninety years of age in the 1920's.

The two wood blocks (below) are by unknown carvers although one bears the initials "CF."

The bird and tulip blocks are by Peter Montelius who established the first printing press in Reamstown, Pennsylvania, around 1809. He later became a schoolmaster in Northumberland county where he also made engravings for a druckery (printing shop) near Sunbury. In recent years broadsides with Montelius blocks have brought as much as $1,400 at folk art and antique auctions. Montelius imprints are very similar in motif and execution to those of G. Miesse of Tulpehocken who carved birds, flowers and angels which illustrated Taufscheins, house blessings and broadsides printed by Johann Ritter of Reading.

The animal wood engravings were used by the Henkel Press, New Market, Virginia. Established in 1806, this was one of the first major German language printers south of the Mason-Dixon line.

The large wood-cut illustration below (approximately 13″ x 9″), was handcrafted in 1968 by John D. Sheppard, an artisan of Lancaster County, Pennsylvania. The scene, used for a commercial advertisement, illustrates the atmosphere of a Pennsylvania Dutch "forbay" barn. Original on display at the Folk Craft Museum, Witmer, Pa.

Wood cuts used on Henkel imprints between 1810 and 1825.

Henkel cuts were from several sources; some were made locally but records indicate purchases were made from Johann Ritter, Reading; and John Gruber, Hagerstown, Maryland; and G. Miesse, an engraver who visited New Market, Virginia.

The Eagle (above) by Schimmel is on display at the Pennsylvania Farm Museum.

Wandering Whittlers

WHITTLING was a leisure activity for some men in early America but few of the results found a market or survived the ravages of time. This is perhaps a reason that it was so very late before any American whittler received recognition. Henry Wilhelm Schimmel was the first noted folk carver and his product was from the 1860's to the 1890's. Schimmel wandered around the Cumberland Valley obtaining food and lodging for his creative efforts—yet he produced a wide assortment of small animal pieces of which his eagles were popular. Many of his carvings were given a coat of gesso (a mixture of plaster of paris and glue or similar materials used as a ground for painting) and brightly painted—these are sometimes referred to as *polychrome sculpture!*

Aaron Mountz (Mounts) was another whittler from the same general geographic area as Schimmel. His product was less extensive in quantity but more finished, and was left unpainted. Mountz never married and stayed on the family farm which was not productively prosperous. Both of these noted carvers died in the Cumberland County almshouse—Schimmel in 1890 and Mountz in 1949.

The small eagle (far left) is covered with gesso and painted; the balled eagle is by an unknown maker and is gilded.

Daniel Strawser, contemporary wood carver from Berks County, Pa., has followed in the folk art tradition, gaining original inspiration from Schimmel pieces. His only instrument is a sharp pocket knife, working on sugar pine, bass wood or ponderosa pine. His wife, Barbara, does the decorating and painting. They annually demonstrate their skill at the Kutztown Folk Festival and the Pennsylvania Farm Museum.

Strawser also fashions some of his birds in the manner of an early Berks County itinerant carver who wandered throughout the area at the turn-of-the-century. Referred to in the dialect as "Schtock-schnitzler (cane carver) Simmons," he carved birds which he attached to sassafras branches by using wire for the bird legs.

Examples of work of the Strawsers are shown above and pictures of Dan carving are below. All of his pieces are marked with the initials "D + BS" with the year and state.

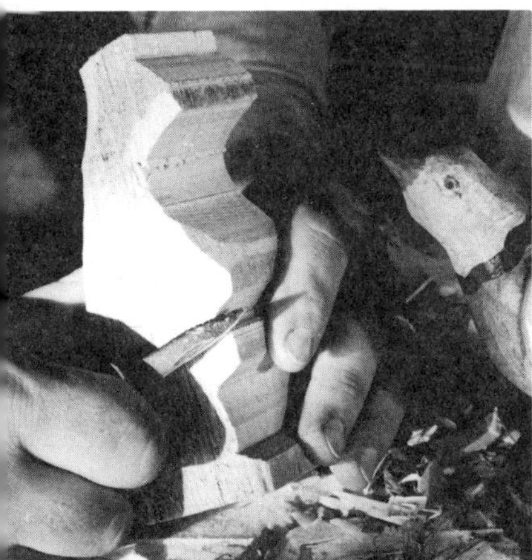

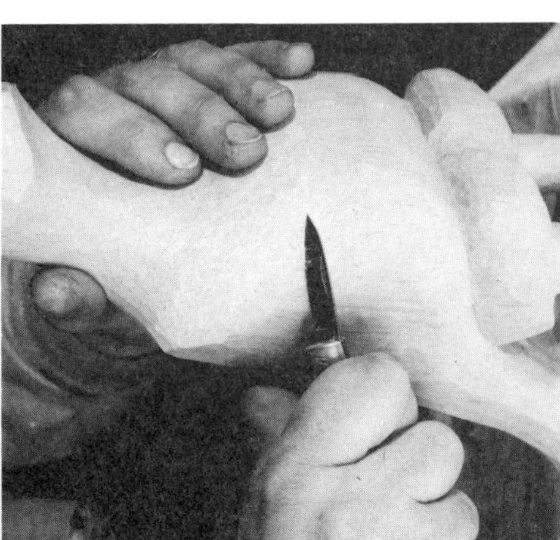

Hand-carved and painted wooden birds, maker unknown, circa 1930 from the Hudson River Valley, New York.

Caricatures of the World War II period, left to right, Hitler, Mussolini, Churchill, Ghandi, Dewey and DeGaulle. From 5″ to 7″ high all solid block in hardwood except Ghandi's glasses!

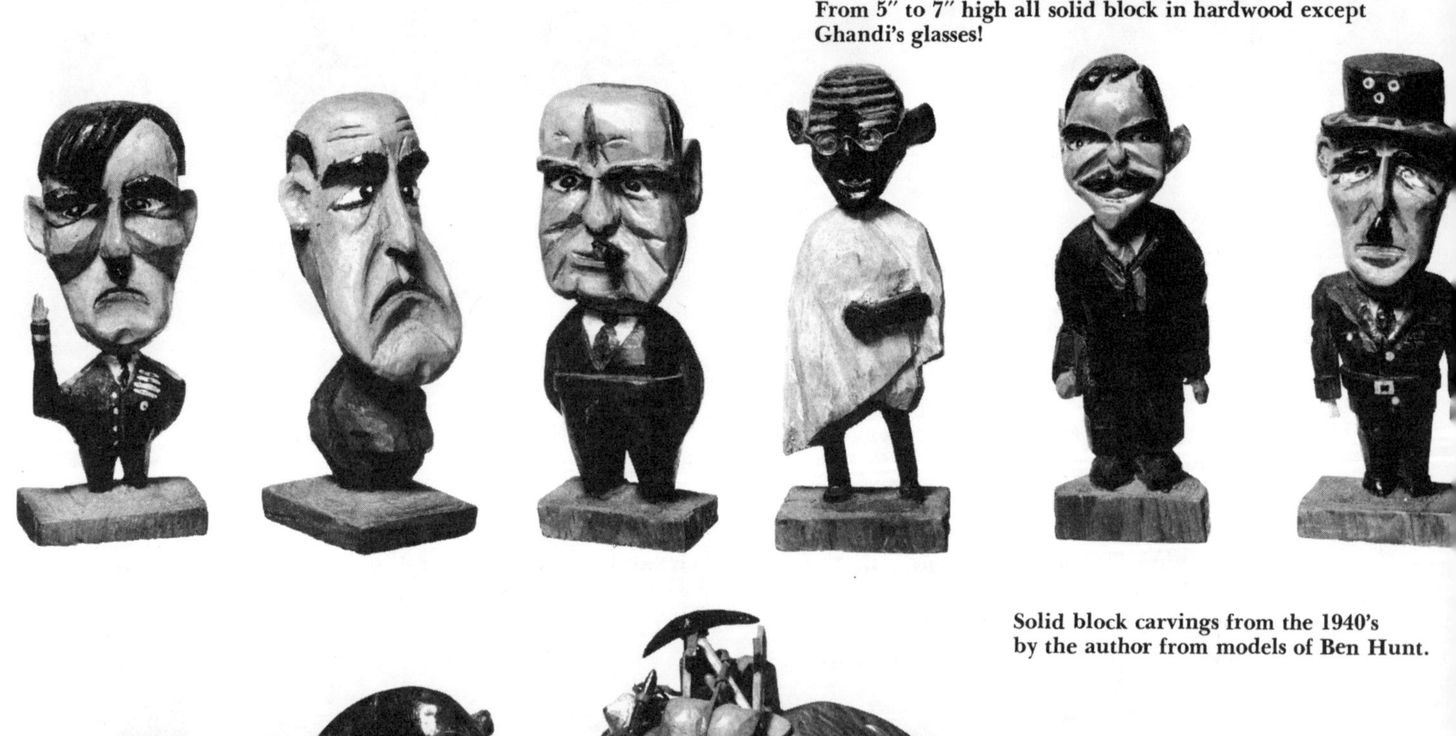

Solid block carvings from the 1940's by the author from models of Ben Hunt.

Unique *watshalycalits* made by Samuel L. Newswenger. The wings are split and fanned out from a single piece of wood!

The specimen below stands on a carved pedestal, the other hangs from a string. Both have bird bodies made separate from the wings and attached.

Carved bird with part of its pedestal missing. Maryland, circa 1870.

Three primitive wooden figures, 3″ tall, from the Appalachian mountains of North Carolina.

The Putz

Covered-bridge 9″ long, made by Adam S. Hahn.

THE HAND-MADE and painted solid block architectural toys are of particular interest because they appear to be in the tradition of the Christmas *Putz* objects. The Putz was an arrangement of objects, usually under a Christmas tree, depicting a farm scene. The custom of making a Christmas scene originated in Italy and became popular in Germany by the beginning of the Eighteenth Century. Carved wooden figures (sometimes in wax, plaster or papier maché) depicted the Holy Family, sheep, oxen, donkey, shepherds and a manger arranged to represent the stall at Bethlehem.

The custom was perpetuated in America as a tradition of the Moravians. It became a seasonal custom at Bethlehem, Pennsylvania.

Village block toys shown below were found in Grant County, West Virginia, where there is a large agrarian population of German heritage.

Although carved wooden objects made in America for the use at a Christmas putz are not known to exist, a number of popular sites appear to have emerged from this practice. *Roadside America,* near Hamburg, Pennsylvania, has been open to the public for many years, where a large structure exhibits model villages, farms and mountain cabins. An entire program is centered around these multiple miniature scenes.

In more recent years, Adam Hahn created *America Wonderland* out of thousands of hand-carved figures, animals and structures—miniature circus parades, schools, churches, horse and carriages, covered bridges—even skyscrapers! His death leaves the future of his display uncertain.

Shown above is one of Adam G. Hahn's scale drawings and products produced for America Wonderland. All carvings and wagon parts are completely handmade. Born in Hamburg (Berks Co.), Pa., he was active as the creator of America Wonderland, Route 272, Denver, Pa.

Miniature walnut wagon jack measuring 6″ made in 1870.

Walnut solid one-piece chairs and miniature three-drawer dresser.

Carved wooden oxen pull a hand-made European type toy plow. From the Hudson River Valley region.

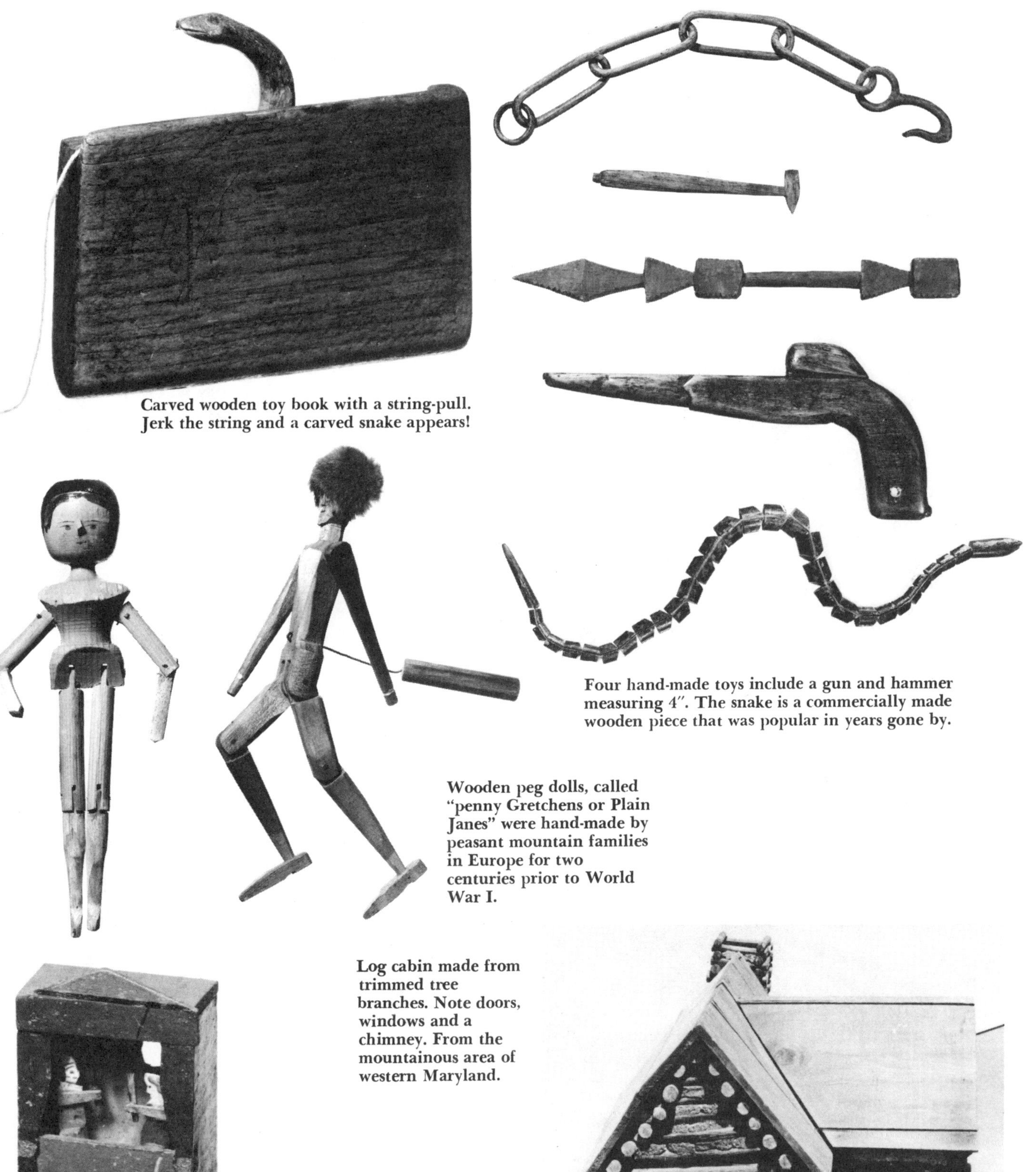

Carved wooden toy book with a string-pull. Jerk the string and a carved snake appears!

Four hand-made toys include a gun and hammer measuring 4″. The snake is a commercially made wooden piece that was popular in years gone by.

Wooden peg dolls, called "penny Gretchens or Plain Janes" were hand-made by peasant mountain families in Europe for two centuries prior to World War I.

Log cabin made from trimmed tree branches. Note doors, windows and a chimney. From the mountainous area of western Maryland.

The tiny "Punch and Judy" actually works! It measures 3½″ tall.

More Carving

THE WIDE RANGE of response to the wood carving urge is shown here. The lantern-like piece with the moveable ball is a real "fun-piece" made in 1900 by a Massanutten mountaineer. To the right the carver came up with *three* free-moving balls.

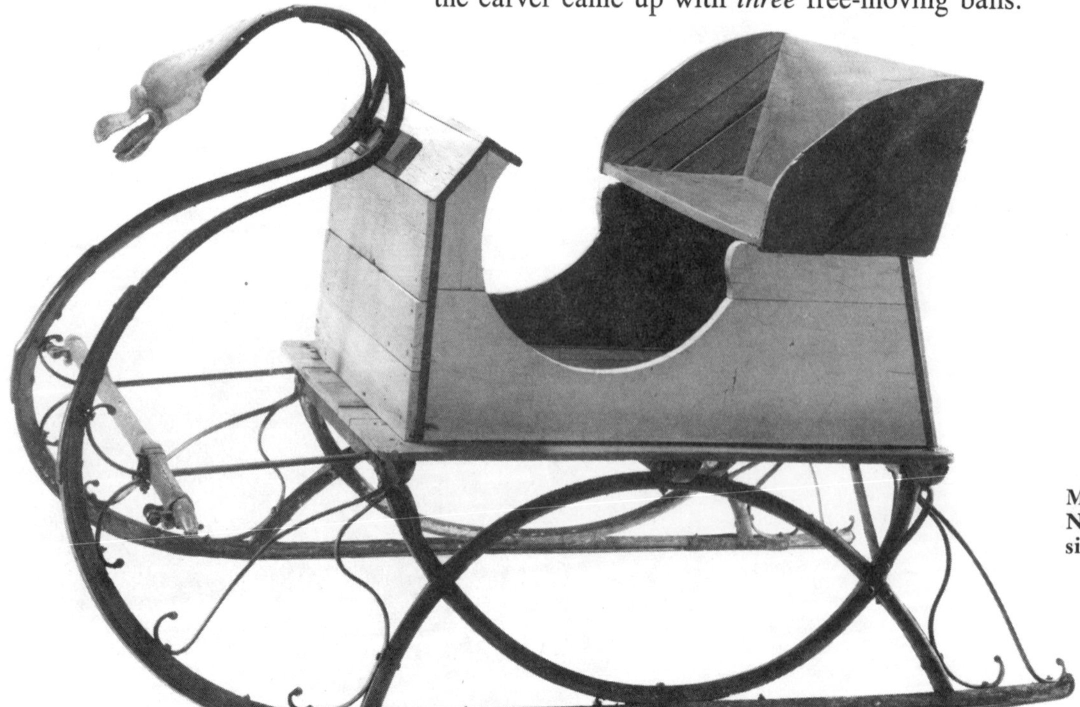

Maple carved pestle, 8″ tall. Note decorated design on the sides.

An unknown Appalachian folk craftsman carved the walnut deer head, graced with real antlers.

Another combination of craftsmanship is this well-executed sleigh with wrought iron runners and hand-carved goose/swan head. From the Page Valley in the Shenandoah area.

Items on pages 27 and 28 are on display in the Folk Craft Museum, Witmer, Pennsylvania.

A farm scene made by Abner Zook shows his unusual three-dimensional technique which laminates carved wood blocks on a wooden backing, giving the impression of depth which emerges with the painting. This little-used style has been applied to small shadow boxes and pictures but seldom in the size and depth created by craftsman Zook.

The small walnut dove-tailed chest has stars and a hand-carved eagle with the initials of the owner.

Bench and Box

THE CHESTNUT carved bench above features bird and flower design with added geometric carvings. This was a real chip-carvers challenge—particularly since it is in chestnut which splits easily. 16½″ tall, 29½″ long. Maker is unknown.

The pine box with carved oak leaves and acorn design measuring 14″ long is a real treasure.

This oak chest below measures 36″ long, 21″ deep and 14″ high, with eleven separately carved panels, each with a different design. The center panel carving features mother and infant in a cradle. New Hampshire, circa 1820.

A Mountain Craft

THE CRAFTS of the southern Appalachians have historically tended to be primarily utilitarian. Limited economic resources and the need for self-sufficiency left little time for the decorative aspects of hand-made objects.

Tourism and the interest in the isolated areas of our nation has, in the last quarter century, created a demand for this hand work of the women folk. Quilts, corn husk, apple head, and hickory nut dolls aroused a widespread interest. One result has been that some men have switched from whittling away time to carving as a cash crop. The specimens shown below are early carvings created for sale to "outlanders." Made of local hardwoods—walnut, ash, apple, maple and cherry—each has the initials of the maker. The lamb and hen are cut out to serve as napkin holders.

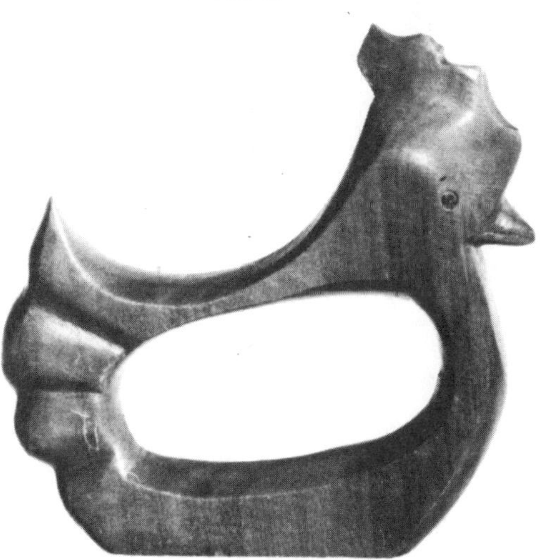

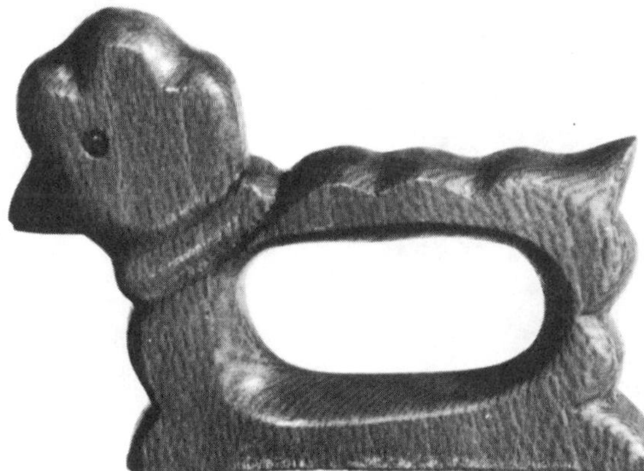

Weather Vanes

THE WHIRLYGIG (above) is hand-carved and the arms whirl merrily in a breeze. The Indian hunter with his dog was originally made by Harry Ruppert. The one illustrated is a replacement made by his son around 1940—even the new one has three feathers missing!

The goose is a unique barn decoration, mounted on a cork perch. Each of the wings is from a natural formed piece of wood that has been trimmed. The fish seems out of his element. Painted red and white, it is 24″ long.